טו בשבט

United Synagogue Commission on Jewish Education

TU BISHVAT

by Norma Simon

Illustrations by Harvey Weiss

Copyright © 1961 by United Synagogue of America—Printed in U.S.A.

Tu Bishvat is a holiday.
Tu Bishvat is a special day.
Tu Bishvat is a planting day
for Jewish children everywhere.

Tu Bishvat is a planting day
for David and for me
and for my friends at school.

In the middle of the orange are the white, smooth seeds.

I take three to school.
Danny and Judy and Aaron and Ann
 all have seeds to plant.

My teacher has paper cups,
    one for every child.
The cup is filled with special,   black   earth
    good for growing things.
We make 3 holes in the soft,   black   earth.
    1   2   3.

We put our seeds inside
 the holes.
   1   2   3.

We cover the holes with earth.
     1   2   3.

Under the earth,   the soft,   black   earth,
  my seeds are beginning to grow.

After we plant our seeds,
our teacher shows us pictures

of children in Israel
on Tu Bishvat,
and they are planting trees.
Flowers are growing,
blossoms are on the trees,
in far away Israel.

In Israel, far, far away,
 spring comes early in the year.
Israeli children plant small trees
 and wait for them to grow.

On the teacher's desk,
 are fruits that grow in Israel.

  Brown dates,
   dried figs,
    round oranges,
     and little raisins.

"What's that, teacher?" I ask.
"Those are figs," my teacher says.
"Would you like to try some?"

We each take a fruit.
I take a fig,   brown, and round, and dry.
Before we take a bite,   we all say a *B'rakhah*.
*Ba-rukh a-tah Ado-nai, Elo-he-nu me-lekh ha-olam,
bo-rey p'ri ha-etz.*

The fig is hard to chew,

and chew,

and chew.

Now I'll try a soft brown date.

When the fruit is finished,
on Tu Bishvat,
it's time to go home
from Hebrew kindergarten.

I carry my seeds home
> inside the cup
> to keep my seeds near the sun,
> to water my seeds every day.

Outside, it's still cold winter,
> but the sun is warm on my window.
The sun is warm on the soft, black earth.

Every day,
   David and I look
   at the soft, black earth.

One day,
   after many, many days,
   David sees something pushing up.
David calls,   "Ruth!"
David calls,   "Mother!"
I call,   "Daddy!"

We want everyone to see
 with David and me.
The seeds I planted are growing up
 just like David and me.

The seeds grow
> just a little at a time
> for days and days,
> for weeks and weeks,
> with water,
> with sun,
> in the soft, black earth.

Two of my seeds come up.
One seed doesn't grow.
The stems grow stronger.
The leaves grow out
    flat,
      shiny,
        green.
The roots grow down
    into the earth.
The stems grow up
    into the light.

We have many plants in my house.
We have many plants in my school.
But my Tu Bishvat plants
    are very special to me,
    and I watch them grow
    in a special way.

Tu Bishvat is a planting day,
    indoors   where I live,
    outdoors   in Israel.
For all Jewish children
    everywhere,
Tu Bishvat is a planting day.

WORDS FOR PRONUNCIATION
AND DEFINITION

Tu Bishvat (Too Bish-VAHT)   The fifteenth day of the Hebrew month of Sh'vat (February, usually).

B'rakhah (B'rah-KHAH)   A blessing or a prayer.